FANTASY

STORY

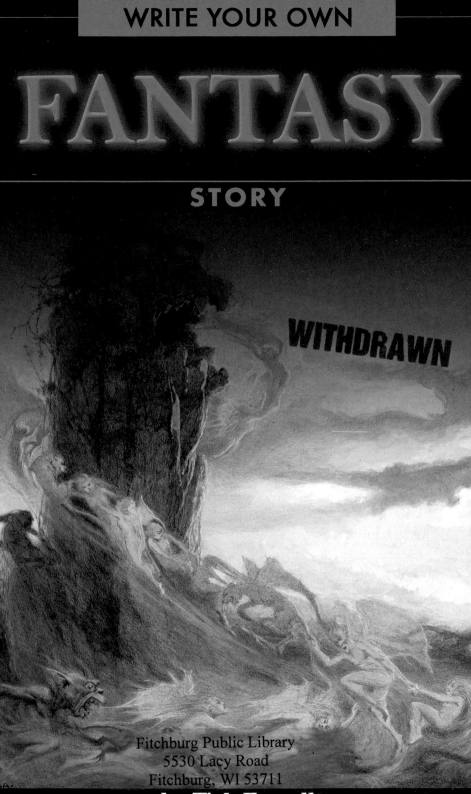

WITHDRAWN

by Tish Farrell

First published in the United States in 2006 by
Compass Point Books
3109 West 50th Street #115
Minneapolis, MN 55410

Copyright © ticktock Entertainment Ltd 2006
First published in Great Britain in 2006 by ticktock Media Ltd.,
ISBN 1 86007 532 0 PB

 This book was manufactured with paper containing
at least 10 percent post-consumer waste.

Visit Compass Point Books on the Internet at
www.compasspointbooks.com
or e-mail your request to
custserv@compasspointbooks.com

For Compass Point Books
Sue Vander Hook, Nick Healy, Anthony Wacholtz, Nathan Gassman, James Mackey,
Abbey Fitzgerald, Catherine Neitge, Keith Griffin, and Carol Jones

For ticktock Entertainment Ltd
Graham Rich, Elaine Wilkinson, John Lingham,
Suzy Kelly, Heather Scott, Jeremy Smith

Library of Congress Cataloging-in-Publication Data
Farrell, Tish.
   Write your own fantasy story / by Tish Farrell.
      p. cm.—(Write your own)
   Includes bibliographical references and index.
   Audience: Grade 4-6.
   ISBN-13: 978-0-7565-1639-0 (hardcover)
   ISBN-10: 0-7565-1639-0 (hardcover)
   ISBN-13: 978-0-7565-1814-1 (paperback)
   ISBN-10: 0-7565-1814-8 (paperback)
   1. Science fiction—Authorship—Juvenile literature.   I. Title.
PN3377.5.F34F37 2006
808.3'8766—dc22   2005033654

Your writing quest

Fantasy stories—from The Wizard of Oz *to* Harry Potter—*feature characters, places, and events that are beyond what is possible in our world. These stories make amazing, surprising, and fantastic things seem completely real. As a fantasy writer, your first challenge is to discover the lost corners of your imagination—to set free the stories that are held captive there. This won't always be easy. You will encounter many challenges and obstacles, but if you follow the advice and exercises in this book, you will gain the skills you need to reach your goal. To help you, there will be tips and guidance from some famous writers and examples from their books to give you more ideas.*

CONTENTS

WANT TO BE A WRITER?

This book is the perfect place to start. It will give you the tools to write your own fantasy story. Learn how to craft believable characters and perfect plots, along with satisfying beginnings, middles, and endings. Examples from a variety of famous books are used with tips and techniques from published authors to help you on your way.

Get the writing habit

Do timed and regular practice. Real writers learn to write even when they don't particularly feel like it.

Create a story-writing zone.

Keep a journal.

Keep a notebook—record interesting events and note how people behave and speak.

Generate ideas

Find a character whose story you want to tell. What is his or her problem?

Brainstorm to find out everything about your character.

Research settings, events, and other characters.

Get a mix of good and evil characters.

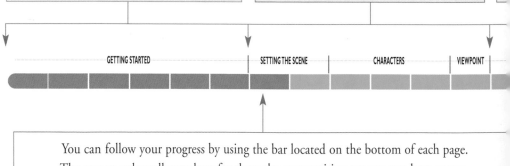

GETTING STARTED   SETTING THE SCENE   CHARACTERS   VIEWPOINT

You can follow your progress by using the bar located on the bottom of each page. The orange color tells you how far along the story-writing process you have gotten. As the blocks are filled out, your story will be growing.

Plan

What is your story about?

What happens?

Plan beginning, middle, and end.

Write a synopsis or create story-boards.

Write

Write the first draft, then put it aside for a while.

Check spelling and dialogue—does it flow?

Remove unnecessary words.

Does the story have a good title and satisfying ending?

Avoid clichés.

Publish

Write or print the final draft.

Always keep a copy for yourself.

Send your story to literary magazines, Internet writing sites, competitions, or school magazines.

SYNOPSES AND PLOTS | WINNING WORDS | SCINTILLATING SPEECH | HINTS AND TIPS | THE NEXT STEP

When you get to the end of the bar, your book is ready to go! You are an author!
You now need to decide what to do with your book and what your next project should be.
Perhaps it will be a sequel to your story, or maybe something completely different.

BEGIN THE FANTASY

First gather your writing materials and find your story-making place. One of the best things about being a writer is that you don't need much equipment. Fantasy writers need only pen and paper to make their magic. A computer can make writing quicker, but it is not essential.

Gather what you need

Apart from a pen and paper, you may also need to use your library and the Internet for research. As you learn your craft, it's also handy to have the following:

- small notebook that you carry everywhere
- colored pencils (think magic wands!) to create your fantasy world
- pens with gold and silver ink to record magical thoughts

- different colored Post-it notes to mark any important book passages or keep track of ideas
- stick-on stars to highlight your best ideas
- files and folders to keep precious story ideas safe
- dictionary, thesaurus, and encyclopedia

Find a writing place

Writers can work wherever they like. Roald Dahl (*The BFG*) and Philip Pullman (His Dark Materials trilogy) wrote in their garden sheds. J. K. Rowling (Harry Potter series) wrote in a café. You may find your bedroom is the best place, or a quiet corner of the library. Experiment. See where you feel most comfortable, and wherever it is, be sure to sit up straight.

Create a story-writing zone

- Play music to encourage magical thoughts.

- Spray an unusual spicy scent.

- Spread out a selection of fantasy pictures.

- Choose some mysterious objects for your writing space—interesting things you've collected from the beach, a quartz crystal, a pure white feather, or whatever else suits you. They should be things that have a story to tell.

Writer's golden rule

Once you have chosen your writing space, the first step in becoming a writer is: Go there as often as possible, and write. You must write and write regularly. This is the writer's golden rule.

Until you are sitting at your desk with pen in hand, no writing can happen. It doesn't matter what you write—an e-mail or a diary entry will do—as long as you write something.

GET THE WRITING HABIT

Before you can conjure duels with dragons or challenge evil magicians, you must get into training. It may sound dull, but it has to be done. The best writers practice writing every day, even when they haven't got a story to tell or don't feel at all inspired. You need to exercise your writing "muscles" in the same way you would train to play football or practice the piano before a performance.

Now it's your turn

Learn to unlock your imagination

Decide in advance how long your first writing practice will be. It could be two minutes to begin with. Now close your eyes, and take four slow, deep breaths. Open your eyes, check the time, and write the phrase "Sword in the Stone" at the top of the page. Then brainstorm. See how many other magical words, names, and phrases you can think of. Write everything that comes into your head. Don't take your pen from the paper. Spew like a volcano. Don't stop until your two minutes are up. Hurray! You've proved you can write.

TIPS AND TECHNIQUES

Make a regular date with your writing desk. Your practice may be five minutes or an hour. The trick is to stick to it.

ARTHUR·AND·THE·QUESTING·BEAST

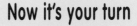

Now it's your turn

Describe your fantasy world

Run your eyes over what you wrote in the previous exercise. Circle five words you like best. Work your five circled words into a description of your ideal fantasy world. Again, don't worry if you write nonsense. This is about becoming a writer, not about being a perfect writer.

When you've finished both practice exercises, give yourself a gold star. You are on your way to finding the Lost Mines of Your Imagination. The more you do exercises like this, the easier it will be to overcome the writer's worst enemy—the Story Specter. This is the voice in your head that continually finds fault with your writing, also called your internal critic.

Brainstorm ideas

Try these story starters:

- *The day it rained broomsticks*
- *How I turned my gerbil/cat/labrador into a handsome prince and the terrible trouble it caused my family*

Also, brainstorming with a friend can be fun. Try writing alternate lines of a story starting:

Once in the heart of a dark forest, a huge green egg began to…

Case study

Eoin Colfer used to be a teacher. Every afternoon after school, and before looking after his little boy, he would grab an hour to work on his first book, the best-selling Artemis Fowl.

All good writing starts with lots of good reading. Before you can write fantasy, you need to know what it is. Like science fiction, fantasy is a genre that often sets its stories in imagined worlds. Fantasy worlds are ruled by magic—usually with wizards or witches who know how to use it. But the magic always has some limitations.

What is fantasy writing?

In fantasy stories, the impossible is always possible. They feature talking animals, trees that come to life, giants and elves, and mountains of fire. They send characters on adventures in strange worlds, but readers can discover important things about human nature and real life by following these fantastic tales.

Read, read, read

Begin by reading as many different fantasy stories as you can find. This will help to develop your own tastes and decide what you want to write about. You will get ideas, too. If something sparks your imagination, write it down in your notebook. Start an "ideas" page.

Discover your tastes

Think more deeply about the books you like. Are they set in totally different worlds, with wizards and magic forces like J. R. R. Tolkien's The Lord of the Rings? Or do you like the story to move back and forth between real and imagined places as in C. S. Lewis' *The Chronicles of Narnia?* Or do you prefer something humorous set in the real world, such as Roald Dahl's *Matilda?*

Look more deeply

Go back to a favorite fantasy story, and as you read, imagine that you are writing it. Start looking for the things that make that world so believable. When you first read it, you probably completely lost yourself in it and forgot all about the real world. Now, try to figure out how the author grabbed your attention.

Get inspired

Have you noticed how fantasy stories draw their ideas from other stories? *The Wizard of Oz, The Hobbit, The BFG,* the Dark Materials trilogy—all have their roots in ancient myths and fairy tales. Tolkien may have had Merlin in mind when he created Gandalf.

Create illusions

As a beginning writer, you want to discover why and how stories work. This is like trying to spot how a magician performs his tricks. Story writing is all about creating illusions. So as you study your favorite stories, look for the specific things that make you think that somewhere—in some other place, space, or time—the magic worlds described in them really did exist.

TIPS AND TECHNIQUES

As you read, think about whose story you want to tell. What kind of world do they live in? Write your ideas down in your notebook, and when you come to write your own story, you will have plenty of characters and places to choose from. Read as many different writers as you can. If you're not enjoying a book, set it aside and start one that does grab you. Get inspired and your ideas will flow.

To become a good writer, it helps to read as much as you can. This is the only way you'll discover your own writer's voice—a style of writing that is uniquely yours. This is not something you learn quickly. Many writers go on developing their voices all their lives.

Finding your writer's voice

Once you start reading with your writer's mind switched on, you will notice that writers have their own rhythm, style, and range of language that stays the same throughout the book. Philip Pullman, author of *Northern Lights*, would never write like Lemony Snicket, author of *A Series of Unfortunate Events*. Harry Potter series creator J. K. Rowling's voice is nothing like *Artemis Fowl* author Eoin Colfer's, even though they both write with humor. Spotting how different writers craft their stories is like recognizing your favorite rock bands, even when they're singing brand-new songs. Of course, you can only find your voice once you start writing stories.

Case study

Eoin Colfer drew inspiration for Artemis Fowl *from Irish history and the wealth of traditional Irish legends.*

TIPS AND TECHNIQUES

Experiment with your reading. Don't just stick to your favorite author. Try books you wouldn't normally read, like a historical novel or real-life story. It may inspire you in ways you don't expect.

WRITERS' VOICES

Look at the kinds of words these authors use. Do they use lots of adjectives? What about the length of their sentences? Which style do you prefer to read?

HANS CHRISTIAN ANDERSEN

The snow-flake grew bigger and bigger, until at last it turned into a lady clothed in the finest white gauze made up of millions of star-like snow-flakes. She was very beautiful, but she was of ice, dazzling, gleaming ice, all through, and yet she was alive.

Hans Christian Andersen, *The Snow Queen*

EOIN COLFER

Commander Root was sucking on a particularly noxious fungus cigar. Several of the Retrieval Squad had nearly passed out in the shuttle. Even the pong from the manacled troll seemed mild in comparison.

Eoin Colfer, *Artemis Fowl*

PHILIP PULLMAN

A cold drench of terror went down Lyra's spine. ... She had one day in which to find Roger and discover whatever she could about this place, and either escape or be rescued; and if all the gyptians had been killed, who would help the children stay alive in the icy wilderness?

Philip Pullman, *Northern Lights*

KATE DiCAMILLO

In the dungeon, there were rats. Large rats. Mean rats. Despereaux was destined to meet those rats. Reader, you must know that an interesting fate awaits almost everyone, mouse or man, who does not conform.

Kate DiCamillo, *The Tale of Despereaux*

If you are stuck for story ideas, don't panic. That will just make your brain go blank. In fact, you already have lots of ideas, locked away in the Lost Mines of Your Imagination. This is where your subconscious memory stores every story experience you ever had.

Free your stories

The true writer's art is to extract all the brilliant story strands that are hidden in his or her head and to shape them into sparkling new tales. Brainstorming is a good way to start accessing your subconscious memory, but you'll probably need some extra tricks, too, before you can free your stories.

Gather material

If you ask writers where they get their ideas, they will say things like "everywhere," or a character "just came to them." In fact, most writers store ideas for years, gathering information both consciously and subconsciously. Things get mixed up with memories and other stories and conversations they overhear. People they meet get mixed in, too, along with newspaper articles, song lyrics, and bits of poems. Everyone does this, but writers do it on purpose. Their brains are like a crow's nest—actively collecting things to recycle later. Once in a while, something triggers a fully formed character or story.

Case study

Author Philip Pullman says he's stolen ideas from every book he's read. By this, he doesn't mean that he copied other writers' works. He means that his own story ideas are often inspired by memories of the things he has read—from comics to poetry to ancient stories.

Now it's your turn

Brainstorm

Speed up your ideas search with this brainstorming exercise. Cut up some scrap paper into 10 squares (big enough to write one name on). Do the same with five different colored sheets of paper, so you end up with six piles of 10 squares. Now you are going to write, as fast as you can, the first thoughts that come into your mind. On your first pile of squares, write the names of 10 possible heroes (such as Witchfinder-Elfgirl), one per square. The other piles are for: the main villain (such as Worst Witch), a name for your fantasy world or a part of it (such as Heights of Horus), a magical object that will be important in the story (such as Truth Wand), a hero's helper (such as Silver Falcon), and a villain's henchman (such as Man-eating Cat).

Now shuffle each pile and place them all face down on your writing desk. Turn over the top square from each pile. You now have the vital ingredients for a fantasy story: heroes, villains, a place, an object for them to battle over, and supporting characters.

TIPS AND TECHNIQUES

Keep your brainstorming notes in your notebook or in a separate file. A lot of it may seem like nonsense now. But the next time you flip through, something may inspire you.

Find more ideas and develop your story

Good stories can take time to emerge. Instead of forcing them, try setting your brain to the task before you go to sleep. Ask your subconscious mind to come up with some ideas. The next day, you may find that your fuzzy thinking has come into sharp focus.

Use facts

Sometimes research is called for. This might sound like an odd thing to do for a fantasy story, but factual accounts of past events can be more extraordinary than fantasy.

• If you want convincing sounding spells, find a book on the history of sorcery and see what new ideas it conjures.

• If you want to create a wonderful castle, research different kinds— English, French, Indian, Chinese—then mix them together with some thoughts of your own. You will have something truly original.

You can use your own technical knowledge, too. If you play a musical instrument, know a lot about computers, play chess, or practice an unusual sport—archery or a martial art—then try blending your own special knowledge with some fantasy characters and see where it takes you. You could suddenly find yourself with a unique story to tell.

Case study

Robert Louis Stevenson said that the idea for his story The Strange Case of Dr. Jekyll and Mr. Hyde *came to him in a dream. Like other well-known writers, he kept a dream diary. Keep a notebook by your bed and write down any good ideas as soon as you wake up—before they burst like bubbles.*

Case study

J. R. R. Tolkien was a professor at Oxford University while he was writing **The Hobbit** and **The Lord of the Rings**. The stories for both books grew out of his knowledge of ancient European languages and the Norse and Icelandic sagas. He reused names and words from these old sources to create his own fabulous mythology.

Once your story ideas start to simmer, help things along by thinking in more detail of the place where the story will take place. Try the exercise in the Now It's Your Turn box again on page 9. Can you feel your ideas developing? Do you need some more…?

TIPS AND TECHNIQUES

Ideas can come from anywhere at anytime. J. K. Rowling had nothing to write on when the idea for the Harry Potter series came to her. She was stuck on a train and that's how the Hogwarts Express was born. Always have your notebook handy.

IMAGINE MAGICAL LANDS

In fantasy books, the setting is as important as the characters. Think of Narnia or Middle Earth. Now imagine your story's setting. What does the countryside look like? What kind of beings inhabit it? Is it a wild, untamed land or is it built up with spired cities? Does your world have different rules from the real world? How will they affect your plot?

Explore new places

You need to know how the places in your world will guide your plot. If your hero needs to go to a special place to complete the quest, then tell the readers something about the place as soon as possible. Use it to build suspense by hinting at the terrible dangers along the way. The more exciting or fantastic you make your geography, the more interesting your story can be.

Case study

Paul Stewart, who wrote the Edge Chronicles says the ideas for the books began with illustrator Chris Riddell's map of the place. After that, the books developed as a joint effort—Chris drawing ideas and Paul writing. See the detailed plans in **Beyond the Deepwoods** *or* **The Curse of the Gloamglozer.**

Case study

Alan Garner set his stories **The Weirdstone of Brisingamen** *and* **The Moon of Gomrath** *in rural Cheshire, England, where he grew up. He studied local myths and got to know the ancient historical places around Alderley Edge. Because they seemed magical to him in real life, they became even more magical when he used them in his stories.*

Now it's your turn

Map your landscape

If you have read The Lord of the Rings trilogy, you'll remember the Mines of Moria, the Dead Marshes, Lothlorien, and Hobbiton. Like Tolkien, you can create your own strange world in fiction. Spend five minutes writing down all the spine-chilling places and monsters that you would like your hero to take on. Now repeat the exercise, listing places with entrancing qualities, such as a crystal spring whose waters bestow powers to see the future. Creating safe havens for your heroes allows them and your readers to catch their breath—or to be lulled into a false sense of security.

Once you know your fantasy world really well, pick out only the most striking things to describe. Think brief. Think sharp. Think exciting. From the start, give them vivid clues to trigger their senses. Have something happening at the same time—something mysterious that snags the reader's curiosity.

Cook up a good setting: Recipe #1

Combine description with action:

> Among the trees something was happening that was not meant for human eyes ... a shaft of blue light cut the darkness. It came from a narrow opening in a high tooth-shaped rock, and within the opening was a pair of iron gates thrown wide, and beyond them a tunnel. Shadows moved on the trees as a strange procession entered through the gates and down into the hill. They were a small people.
>
> Alan Garner, *The Moon of Gomrath*

Recipe #2

Combine description with action from a character's point of view:

> Holly rolled off her futon and stumbled into the shower. That was one advantage of living near the earth's core—the water was always hot. No natural light, of course, but that was a small price to pay for privacy. Underground. The last human-free zone. There was nothing like coming home from a long day on the job, switching off your shield and sinking into a bubbling slime pool. Bliss.
>
> Eoin Colfer, *Artemis Fowl*

A striking opening

Write the opening paragraph to your story, and see how you can mix setting descriptions with action. Choose words that sizzle—instead of your character walking away, make him flee, fly, or speed through the Grim Gorge. Think of striking images, like Alan Garner's tooth-shaped rock, which creates a very sinister atmosphere. Think of using telling adjectives, too. *Sparkling* is stronger than *shiny*—sparkling does, but shiny just is.

Recipe #3

Combine description with action from a character's point of view and make them in a hurry:

> *Holly grabbed the remains of a nettle smoothie from the cooler and drank it in the tunnels. As usual there was chaos in the main thoroughfare. Airborne sprites jammed the avenue like stones in a bottle. The gnomes weren't helping either, lumbering along with their big swinging behinds blocking two lanes. Swear toads infested every damp patch, cursing like sailors.*
>
> Eoin Colfer, *Artemis Fowl*

Recipe #4

If your fantasy world needs a lot of explanation, write a one-page prologue instead. Use this to set the scene and you won't have to use too much description later on. Tolkien uses prologues in both *The Hobbit* and The Lord of the Rings. From the Edge Chronicles, *The Curse of the Gloamglozer* begins:

> *Far, far away, jutting out into the emptiness beyond, like the figurehead of the mighty stone ship, is the Edge.*
>
> Paul Stewart and Chris Riddell,
> *The Curse of the Gloamglozer*

Andrew Bradford Clarke
Danielle Elizabeth Frederick
Gayle Heather Ireland
Jessica Kathryn Lewis
Michael Nathan O'Connell
Paul Q. Robinson
Stephen Taylor Underhill
Victoria Welch Young
Zachary X. Anderson

DISCOVER YOUR HERO

When writers start their stories they learn about their heroes (protagonists) as they write. Getting to know your characters is like getting to know a new friend. The main thing is that you must care deeply about them, otherwise you won't be able to make the readers care about them.

Find the perfect name

Philip Pullman says Lyra from *Northern Lights* stepped into his mind fully formed, name and all. J. K. Rowling collects words she likes the sound of. Dumbledore means bumblebee in Old English. If you're stuck, flip through a baby names book, an atlas index, or a telephone book. If you make up a name, say it out loud to see what it sounds like.

TIPS AND TECHNIQUES

Start a "special words" list in your notebook. Write down any word that catches your imagination. You'll know where to look the next time you are stuck for a name. Don't make it too complicated for readers to remember. Simple names like Kit, Gem, or Will can often be more memorable.

Build up a picture

You need to know what your hero looks like. Think about his or her clothing, hair, height, build, likes, and dislikes. Is your hero really good at something? What are his or her weaknesses? Think how those weaknesses might play a part in your story. For instance, Lyra is a liar. She also lacks imagination. But both of these flaws often help her out of tough situations.

Now it's your turn

Know your hero

Your heroes need a past. Brainstorm everything you can think of in five minutes—who they are, where they live, whether they have a family, whether they go to work or school. Here is Eoin Colfer's brief history of Holly Short in *Artemis Fowl*:

Technically she was an elf, fairy being a general term. She was a leprechaun too, but that was just a job. ... Cupid was her great-grandfather. Her mother was a European elf with a fiery temper and a willowy frame.

What's the problem?

Finally, and most important, your hero needs a problem. Or several. No one wants to read stories about people with perfect, happy lives. In the Harry Potter series, Harry's life is darkened by his cruel relatives, the Dursleys. Use your own experiences to make your hero's problems real. Your readers will only keep reading if they feel for your characters. You must describe some real emotions. Tap into your own.

CREATE YOUR VILLAIN

Just as your hero must have problems to deal with, your villain must provide the external problem or conflict. So who is your villain? Does the one you dealt yourself in the brainstorming exercise back on page 15 look promising?

Uncover the face of evil

First, think about what makes your villains so evil. Are they hungry for power? Do they want great wealth or some special knowledge that will help them control everyone or will make them immortal? Are they simply cruel and get their pleasure from destroying things? Are they envious of your hero—a rival for some title or position? Abandoned as a young child? Reared by uncaring guardians? Or has it simply never occurred to them to be good?

Now it's your turn

Know your villain

In a 10-minute practice, brainstorm your villain. How does he or she operate and what is his or her motivation? Think about his or her weaknesses, too, and how these might help the story. For example, in the Harry Potter books, Voldemort understands only love of power and not love itself.

Villainous Profiles

MINDLESS EVIL

In The BFG, *Roald Dahl has nine man-eating giants who think their grim behavior is perfectly fine.*

LURKING EVIL

Then there are other evil beings that we hardly see, like Philip Ridley's giant crocodile, Krindlekrax, who inhabits the sewers of Lizard Street. Or Terry Pratchett's rat king, Spider, who tries to melt Maurice's brain in The Amazing Maurice and His Educated Rodents.

SUBTLE VILLAINS

Finally, there are villains who are hard to spot because they are so charming, such as the beautiful Mrs. Coulter in Philip Pullman's The Golden Compass. *This villain hardly ever gives herself away, and the hero, an orphan named Lyra, is shocked to discover Mrs. Coulter's secrets, including the fact that Mrs. Coulter is her mother.*

WORLD DOMINATION

Sauron in The Lord of the Rings *is one of the most frightening villains ever. He is too evil to be wholly described. He shows the results of his evil, too—the terrifying Black Riders and Orcs, the once good Saruman corrupted, the miserable Gollum, and the grim desolation of Mordor.*

TIPS AND TECHNIQUES

The more you question your villains, the more you'll find out about them and the more intriguing they'll become. The most frightening thing of all is something that you can't quite see. The more complex your villain, the bigger the battle for your hero and the more exciting your story.

In fantasy, as in real life, your heroes will be judged by the company they keep. Scenes between the hero and friends are a good way to show the reader what he or she is really like as a person. How would we know how loyal Harry Potter is without seeing him with his friends?

Show the mark of a character

In The Lord of the Rings, Frodo seems an unlikely hero to take on the impossible quest against the mighty Sauron. One way that Tolkien makes us think that he has hidden qualities is by showing us his friend Sam's unshakable devotion to him.

Good guys and bad guys

So when thinking about your cast of characters, you will need good guys and bad guys to help or harm your hero. In the brainstorming exercise on page 15, you dealt yourself a hero's helper and a villain's henchman. Can you now develop these ideas? Make up your own beings, or adapt some from a host of marvelous fantasy creatures in myths and fairy tales. What about a winged horse like Pegasus who might whisk your hero from a crumbling mountaintop in the nick of time, or some variation on the snake-headed Medusa from Greek mythology, who could turn a person to stone by looking at her?

TIPS AND TECHNIQUES

For extraordinary creatures, find a Dictionary of World Mythology in the library. See what ideas you can use. In Artemis Fowl, the fairyland security expert is a centaur—half-man, half-horse. The mix of old with new can make a wonderfully original character.

Now it's your turn

CETUS
ARGUS
SPHINX
MEDUSA

Picture your characters

In your next practice, try sketching your characters. Ask your creations what special powers they have and how these will make your story more exciting. Hunt for good names that tell the reader something about the character. Remember that your characters each need some special quality or flaw that will make them instantly more marvelous or dastardly.

Concoct creatures

A creature from Greek mythology has the hind parts of a dragon, the body of a goat, the front legs of a lion, and the head of each. Mix in equally and—abracadabra!—you have a Chimeara. Can you come up with any scary creature combinations? Tyrannosaurus Rex meets giant vampire bat meets … ?

Now it's your turn

It's all in a name

If your slimy, smelly monster still needs a name, do a two-minute brainstorm, writing down the most disgusting nouns and adjectives you can think of. Pick out the best ones and juggle the letters—"skunk" mixed with "gunge" could make "skunge." Author Brian Jacques plays with words like this to make names. He says hard sounds like "Y" and "G" are good for bad guys.

CHOOSE A POINT OF VIEW

Before you write your opening line, you need to decide if you want to tell the story from one particular person's point of view—say, your hero? Or do you want your readers to know everything that is happening to all your characters at once?

Choose your point of view

The omniscient view

Most fantasy stories and fairy tales are written using the omniscient—or all-seeing—view. This means you can tell readers how the hero feels when he is locked up in the dungeon, what his jailer thinks as he snaps the chains shut, and then describe the blast of dragon's breath that is burning down the East Tower, which neither the hero nor the jailer can see, but you, the author, can. In *A Series of Unfortunate Events*, Lemony Snicket uses the all-seeing view in a way that adds to the dark humor of the stories. J. R. R. Tolkien, C. S. Lewis, and Roald Dahl do the same, showing us what all their different characters are feeling and thinking.

> *It was an unpleasant evening. Lucy was miserable and Edmund was beginning to feel his plan wasn't working as well as expected. The two older children were beginning to think that Lucy was out of her mind. They stood in the passage talking ...in whispers long after she had gone to bed.*
>
> C. S. Lewis, *The Lion, the Witch and the Wardrobe*

The third-person view

Another way to tell the story is from your hero's point of view. This is usually written in the third person past tense. You can write it from the viewpoints of different characters, too. Many stories are told from two viewpoints, set down in alternating chapters, and this can add suspense, especially if one character's viewpoint breaks off at a critical moment or cliffhanger. In Cynthia Voigt's *The Wings of a Falcon*, the story opens from the point of view of a nameless boy. Instantly, we are right inside his head, sharing his fears:

> *He knew from the first that this man would know how to hurt him. He had to keep the fear secret, and he couldn't cry no matter how much he wanted to.*
> Cynthia Voigt, *The Wings of a Falcon*

The first-person view

The first-person point of view can be an exciting way of telling a story. When you say "I did this" or "I saw that," it's much easier to persuade the reader that everything you say is true. But it is no longer possible to know what the other characters are thinking, except when they are talking:

> *Tumber Hill! It's my clamber-and-tumble-and-beech-and-bramble hill! Sometimes, when I'm standing on the top, I fill my lungs with air and I shout. I shout!*
> Kevin Crossley-Holland, *The Seeing Stone*

Now it's your turn

Find your point of view

Write a scene from your own story. Describe your hero battling with some villain. First, write it as the omniscient, all-knowing narrator. Then rewrite it in the third person, from your hero's or villain's viewpoint. Finally, try it in the first person. Read your efforts aloud to yourself. Which one do you prefer and why?

TELL YOUR STORY'S STORY

When your story starts bubbling fiercely in your mind, it's a good idea to write a few paragraphs about it. Tell the story of your story. This is your synopsis and will help you keep your story on track. Tell just enough to be intriguing, but don't give away the story's ending.

To get some ideas, look at the back covers of some fantasy books and read the blurb. See how it says just enough about the hero, villain, and all the problems to make the reader want to read more? They convey tone, too, indicating whether the book is serious or humorous. The blurb from *Johnny and the Dead* by Terry Pratchett conjures up a menacing air:

Not many people can see the dead (not many would want to). Twelve-year old Johnny Maxwell can. And he's got bad news for them: the council want to sell the cemetery as a building site. But the dead aren't going to take it lying down ... especially since it's Halloween tomorrow.

In *The Tale of Despereaux* by Kate DiCamillo, the blurb tantalizes the reader with the various strands of the story:

Here, reader, is the tale of tiny, sickly mouse with unusually large ears. ... It is a tale of impossible love, of bravery and old-fashioned courage. And, reader, it is a tale of treachery; unlimited treachery. It is the Tale of Despereaux ...

Now it's your turn

Write your blurb

Sum up your story in a single striking sentence, then develop it in two or three short paragraphs. Think about your potential readers and try to draw them in to make them want to read the book.

Make a story map

Now you have a synopsis that says what your story is about; a cast of characters; a setting; and you know from whose viewpoint you wish to tell the tale. A useful tool is a story map.

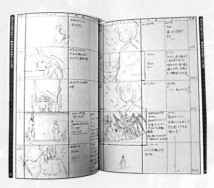

Plan your story scenes

Before filmmakers can start filming, they must know the main story episodes and decide how they can best tell their story in filmed images. To help them, they map out the plot (the sequence of events) in a series of sketches called storyboards. You can do this for your story. Draw the main episodes in pictures. Add a few notes that say what is happening in each scene.

TIPS AND TECHNIQUES

If you can't sum up your story as simply as these excerpts, it is possibly too complicated. Simplify it. As you work on your own synopsis, start asking yourself, "Whose story is this and how will I tell it?"

Create a synopsis

Before they start writing, novelists often list all their chapters, like below, saying briefly what will happen in each chapter or episode. This is called a chapter synopsis, and it provides writers with a skeleton of the plot—which, like the general synopsis, keeps them on track as they write.

A famous example

Here are some storyboard captions for *Peter Pan* by J. M. Barrie. This story first became famous as a play, but it is also a novel.

1. Peter Pan sneaks in to listen to the Darling children's bedtime stories.
2. Peter teaches Wendy, John, and Michael to fly and takes them to Neverland.
3. Egged on by a jealous Tinkerbell, the Lost Boys shoot at Wendy.
4. Peter banishes Tinkerbell for a week and tells the Lost Boys he has brought Wendy to look after them.
5. Captain Hook wants revenge on Peter who cut off his arm and threw it to the crocodile.
6. Peter rescues Tiger Lily at Marooners' Rock; she and her tribe become his ally.
7. Wendy wants to go home and take the Lost Boys.
8. Pirates capture Wendy and the boys.
9. Peter saves them all and Hook is eaten by the crocodile.
10. The children take the Lost Boys home, but Peter Pan stays in Neverland.

TIPS AND TECHNIQUES

Don't let a novel's length put you off from starting one. If you use the story map approach, a novel can be easier to write than a good short story.

GETTING STARTED · SETTING THE SCENE · CHARACTERS · VIEWPOINT

Novels versus short stories

Novels aren't short stories made longer, but short stories made deeper. They still have beginnings, middles, and ends, along with heroes with problems and conflicts, but the main story is expanded with subplots and many more characters and incidents. If you choose to write a novel, a chapter synopsis will help you map out the plot and decide which characters you will need to develop the story. Each chapter heading is then spun out, like a mini-story inside the larger story. In a novel, there is much more room to develop your characters and show the details of their lives, as well as plenty of scope for action scenes and plot twists. Dividing the story into chapters also helps build suspense. If you end a chapter on a cliffhanger with your hero in a perilous situation, and then switch to another character's story in the next chapter, you will have your readers hooked.

Reduce a novel

If you want to write a short story, then mapping out the key scenes like the *Peter Pan* example will also help you pace your story and focus on the most exciting events and characters. It may also identify any flaws in your plot, so you can fix them before you start writing. For example, a short story version of *Peter Pan* would probably cut out some of the scenes and develop Peter Pan's character in more detail.

Now it's your turn

Weave a story web

If you are struggling with your story map, try this exercise.

In the middle of a large piece of paper, draw a rough sketch of your hero within a circle. As you are drawing, imagine that you are that hero, trying to decide which way to go. Think about the problems the hero has and what can be done about them. Draw six spokes extending from your hero circle. Each should lead to another circle. Inside these circles, sketch a different scene or write notes. Each circle will be some new course of action that your hero might take or some obstacle that an enemy sets in your hero's path. Give yourself 20 minutes. You may be surprised how your story starts growing.

BAIT THE HOOK

You have planned your plot and are ready to start telling your own story. Focus on your hero. How will you win the readers to their cause?

Hook your readers

The first part of your story often introduces the main characters, shows your readers the problems and conflicts, and starts the heroes off on their quest to resolve all their difficulties. As you write the opening scenes, imagine you are trying to convince your friends to join you on a hazardous journey. Pull out all the stops.

But where to start your story exactly? What is the opening scene? In *The Wizard of Oz,* the external conflict is very dramatic. No sooner have we learned all about the grayness of Dorothy's Kansas life than the cyclone hits and blows her and Toto away. But by showing a little of what happened before, which is called the back story, the writer creates more drama when the conflict actually comes. J. R. R. Tolkien begins The Lord of the Rings interestingly and a little strangely:

> *When Mr. Bilbo Baggins of Bag End announced that he would shortly be celebrating his eleventy-first birthday with a party of special magnificence, there was much talk and excitement in Hobbiton.*
> J. R. R. Tolkien,
> *The Fellowship of the Ring*

Good beginnings

In *The Bad Beginnings*, writer Lemony Snicket starts by giving readers a challenge they can't resist, as well as making them wonder what story could possibly be so awful?

If you are interested in stories with happy endings, you would be better off reading some other book. In this book, not only is there no happy ending, there is no happy beginning and very few happy things in the middle.

Lemony Snicket, *The Bad Beginnings*

Eoin Colfer has another kind of hook in *Artemis Fowl.* For some reason, the story seems to have started without us.

Ho Chi Min City in the summer. Sweltering by anyone's standards. Needless to say, Artemis Fowl would not have been willing to put up with such discomfort if something extremely important had not been at stake. Important to the plan.

Eoin Colfer, *Artemis Fowl*

TIPS AND TECHNIQUES

Hooking your readers should start from your story's first sentence and paragraph. Study as many story openings as you can find. Which ones work best and why? Make your opening mysterious, dramatic, or funny. Write it and re-write it. Read it aloud. Introduce the conflict in the first sentence or soon afterward. Send your heroes on their way.

BUILD THE SUSPENSE

If beginnings must grip your readers, then middles should grip harder. Find ways to add more complications. Start growing your story by increasing the conflicts.

How to build suspense and excitement

False happy endings

One way to create tension and drama is to have a false happy ending. This is when the hero thinks he or she has solved a problem or defeated a villain, and everyone breathes a sigh of relief. This makes it doubly scary when the enemy rears his ugly head once more. Also, readers start wondering if the hero will fail to defeat the villain next time, too.

Character conflict

Misunderstandings between the characters can add drama and thicken the plot. Perhaps a supporting character has started something that the hero doesn't know about—some kind act that goes wrong, or a deliberate act of betrayal. In *The Lion, the Witch and the Wardrobe* by C. S. Lewis, the early part of the story is about a girl called Lucy trying to make her siblings, Susan and Peter, believe that she has been to another world called Narnia. Next comes the second storyline of brother Edmund's meeting with the White Witch. His denials make things worse for Lucy. Edmund's subplot adds suspense to the main story, driving it on at a more exciting pace. It also adds complications to the sibling relationships and makes the reader wonder how they will be resolved. When all four children step through the wardrobe, Edmund's nasty game is exposed and seemingly resolved, until someone sneaks off to betray all!

Maintain the action

Keep your characters busy at all times—on the move, working things out, coming to the wrong conclusions, having fights, escaping disasters. Think of Harry, Hermione, and Ron trying to save the Sorcerer's Stone:

> *They seized a broomstick each and kicked off into the air, soaring into the midst of the cloud of keys. They grabbed and snatched but the bewitched keys darted and dived ...*
>
> J. K. Rowling, *Harry Potter and the Sorcerer's Stone*

TIPS AND TECHNIQUES

Action scenes should spring from the characters' own plans, not from your need to revive a flagging story. But when you do include them, make them as exciting as possible.

Explore your hero's weaknesses

Using your hero's weaknesses can add more twists and suspense to the story. In *Artemis Fowl*, Holly Short has been so busy with her career that for four years, she has put off performing the ritual to renew her fairy power. Anxious not to lose face, she lies to her boss about this, so she is running low on power when she is sent on a dangerous mission to track an escaped troll. The mission almost goes wrong, giving Artemis Fowl the chance he needs to snatch a leprechaun with her defenses down.

In the last part of your story, the hero's problems must reach a dramatic climax. After this, the problems will be resolved. The story will end, usually with a reference to the story's beginning. Your hero may go back to the old life that readers saw at the story's start, but something important will have changed.

Avoid being predictable

Most readers like a happy ending of some sort, and this is perhaps the hardest part of story writing. You must satisfy your readers' need for this without being predictable.

Count the cost

Your heroes will have gained and learned something, but they might have lost something, too. In J. R. R. Tolkien's *The Return of the King*, the climax of Frodo's story occurs at Mount Doom, where the ring is finally destroyed. How it happens is an unexpected twist, but the quest is a success and the evil Sauron has been defeated. But things are not so simple. Frodo has paid a high price for this victory. He can't go back to his old cozy life in the Shire. It is Sam who goes back to rescue the Shire, taking the story back to where it started—the same place, but no longer the same conditions.

Now it's your turn

Choose your own ending

Read the ending of your favorite fantasy book and then think about what you liked about it and what you didn't. Would you have ended the story differently? If so, how? If you do change it, return to your version later and reread it. Do you still think you are right?

End by suggesting a new beginning

Upbeat endings that suggest more story make readers happy. In *Harry Potter and the Sorcerer's Stone*, the climax comes with Harry's defeat of Voldemort. Then Rowling returns us to where the story started: face to face with the dreadful Dursleys. But before it turns into an anti-climax, she lets readers know that Harry is indeed older and wiser. When Hermione wishes him a good vacation, he shocks her by saying, "They don't know that we're not allowed to use magic at home. I'm going to have a lot of fun with Dudley this summer." The readers grin at the thought of Harry getting some revenge.

Bad endings are ones that:

• fizzle out because you've run out of ideas

• rely on some coincidence or surprise magic that hasn't been mentioned earlier in the story

• fail to show how the characters have changed in some way

    • are too grim and depressing and leave the reader with no hope

TIPS AND TECHNIQUES

Good stories may seem to go in straight lines—beginning, middle, and end—but they also go around in circles. The ending should always have some link with the beginning.

MAKE YOUR WORDS WORK

Words are precious and, like magic wishes, are best used sparingly. When you write, make each word work hard for your story. Use the most vivid or powerful words you can think of.

Write like a charm

All of these devices and more can be used to make your dialogue sparkle:

Use vivid imagery

In *The Seeing Stone*, Kevin Crossley-Holland uses many unusual similes and metaphors. The beech trees sound "like whispering spirits." Merlin has "slateshine eyes," while Lady Alice's are "the color of ripe hazelnuts." When he writes that Ygerna is "so frozen with grief she cannot even melt into tears," we know that she is feeling truly terrible.

Change the length of your sentences

The length of your sentences will set the pace of your story. A variety of sentence lengths will keep readers moving along. You may want to use longer sentences as you create pieces of description or as you explain mounting tension. Shorter sentences will add impact to your surprises. Imagine yourself creeping up on your reader. Then strike.

> It was a unicorn all right, and it was dead. ... Harry had taken one step towards it when a slithering sound made him freeze where he stood. A bush on the edge of the clearing quivered. ... Then out of the shadows, a hooded figure came crawling like some stalking beast...
>
> J. K. Rowling, *Harry Potter and the Sorcerer's Stone*

TIPS AND TECHNIQUES

Action scenes should stick to the action and should not be too drawn out. Use short, punchy phrases and limit description to the bare minimum. Try ending a dramatic scene on a cliffhanger. Leave your heroes in peril and drive your readers to find out what happens next.

Change the mood

Changes in mood can increase or decrease drama, as well as give readers some variety. Tolkien has written much of The Lord of the Rings in a doom-laden tone, but if it were like this from start to finish, the sense of doom would lose its power and the readers' interest. To avoid this, Tolkien weaves in many happier, lighthearted episodes, full of enchantment, which give readers a rest from the high tension. Also, when evil rears its head again, it seems so much worse after the pleasant interlude.

Crank up drama and suspense

Foreshadowing is an essential tool in all fiction writing. It means dropping hints about coming events. In the Harry Potter books, remarks about the fate of Harry's family are used to remind us of Voldemort, sometimes with just a hint of worry, sometimes to stir up some real fear. And whenever Harry's scar starts throbbing, we know Voldemort is on the prowl.

Use dramatic irony

Dramatic irony is another useful device. This is where the reader knows something important that the characters don't know . In *A Series of Unfortunate Events*, Lemony Snicket uses dramatic irony in all his stories—warning us of the horrible things that are going to happen, just when the characters are having a moment's happiness.

USE DRAMATIC DIALOGUE

Dialogue is your chance to bring your creations to life. Your readers can hear your characters' own voices, plus dialogue breaks up a page of narrative (storytelling) and gives readers' eyes a rest. It is a powerful storytelling tool—one that can add color, pace, mood, and suspense to your story.

Let your characters speak for themselves

The best way to learn about dialogue is to switch on your listening ears and eavesdrop. Tune in to the way people choose their words. Write down any good expressions—someone saying "get lost" or "shove off" instead of "go away." Watch people's body language, too, when they are whispering or arguing. Look, listen, and absorb.

Now it's your turn

The art of conversation

Tune in to a TV or radio talk show. Spend 10 minutes writing down what people say, including all the um's, er's, and repetition of points. Listen for a range of voices: young, old, angry, bitter, wise, or dim-witted. Compare what you hear with some dialogue in a book. You will see at once that written dialogue does not include all the hesitations of natural speech. These would be very tedious to read. Fictional dialogue represents real speech, but it does not precisely imitate real speech.

TIPS AND TECHNIQUES

When writing dialogue, stick to "he said" or "she said" for your tags most of the time, but use words like "asked," "cried," or "whispered" to create some variety or to suit the situation in your story.

ollow convention

The way dialogue is written down follows certain rules. It is common to start a new paragraph with every new speaker. What the speaker says is enclosed in quotation marks, followed by a tag such as "he said" or "she said." Other information may be added, including the speaker's feelings, gestures, or actions. Inserting tags in the middle of some speech lines gives the impression of a real conversation. When read aloud, this actually creates a rhythmic flow that makes the exchanges easier to follow. New writers often use alternatives to "said" to avoid repetition, but see how Kate DiCamillo is happy to repeat it.

> *"Would it be possible for me to have a last word with the princess?"*
> *Despereaux asked.*
> *"A word?" said the second hood. "You want a word with a human?"*
> *"I want to tell her what happened to me."*
> *"Geez," said the first hood. He stopped and stamped a paw on the*
> *floor in frustration. "Cripes. You can't learn, can you?"*
> Kate DiCamillo, *The Tale of Despereaux*

Now it's your turn

Write a good argument

Remember an argument you had or heard. Fictionalize it. Change the names but pour anger into the words. Don't rely on dialogue tags like "yelled" or "screamed" to show the mood. Think that the speakers are trying to hurt each other. Their words will fire off like bullets or build quietly to a fatal blow, depending on the character. When you have finished, read it aloud. Now revise it. Take out any unnecessary tags. Cut down all the spoken words to the bare bones, then read it aloud once more. You are learning another absolutely essential writing skill—the art of editing your own work.

USE DRAMATIC DIALOGUE

Fictional eavesdropping

Details about a place or your character's history and motivation can be told much more swiftly in a conversation between two characters. It is more interesting—as any eavesdropping always is, even the fictional sort. In J. M. Barrie's *Peter Pan*, the conversation between Smee and Captain Hook briefly explains Hook's hatred for Peter Pan:

> "I have often," said Smee, "noticed your strange dread of crocodiles."
> "Not of crocodiles," Hook corrected him, "but of that one crocodile. It liked my arm so much, Smee, that it has followed me ever since, from sea to sea and from land to land, licking its lips for the rest of me."
> "In a way," said Smee, "it's a sort of compliment."
> "I want no such compliments," Hook barked petulantly. "I want Peter Pan, who first gave the brute its taste for me."
> J. M. Barrie, *Peter Pan*

Create atmosphere

Dialogue can be used to create different atmospheres. In *The Curse of the Gloamglozer*, the words of Linius Pallitax, the Most High Academe, create both immediate suspense and a sense of bad things to come:

> "And close the door," Linius added. His voice dropped to an urgent whisper. "I don't want a single word of what I'm about to say to go beyond these four walls. Is that understood?"
>
> Paul Stewart and Chris Riddell, *The Curse of the Gloamglozer*

Give direct opinions

If you are writing from a limited viewpoint (third- or first-person), then using dialogue is the only way that readers can hear other characters' opinions directly. Terry Pratchett does this well in the Johnny Maxwell trilogy, where the stories are told from Johnny's viewpoint. He uses dialogue to express the characters' views of each other. In the following extract, Johnny takes Wobbler, Bigmac, and Yo-less to the cemetery to prove he can see dead people:

> *"I don't know as this is right," said Wobbler, when the four of them had gathered by the gate.*
> *"There's crosses all over the place," said Yo-less.*
> *"Yes, but I'm an atheist," said Wobbler.*
> *"Then you shouldn't believe in ghosts—"*
> *"Post-living citizens," Bigmac corrected him.*
> *"Bigmac?" said Johnny.*
> *"Yeah?"*
> *"What're you holding behind your back?" Wobbler craned to see.*
> *"It's bit of sharpened wood," he reported. "And a hammer."*
> *"Bigmac!"'*
>
> Terry Pratchett, *Johnny and the Dead*

TIPS AND TECHNIQUES

As you write your own stories, be on the lookout for description or explanatory passages that would be better as dialogue. Dialogue is never idle chitchat. It moves the story on, by revealing the characters and their circumstances, and speeding up the storytelling.

USE DRAMATIC DIALOGUE

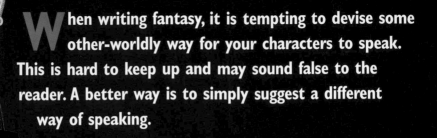

When writing fantasy, it is tempting to devise some other-worldly way for your characters to speak. This is hard to keep up and may sound false to the reader. A better way is to simply suggest a different way of speaking.

Poetic speech patterns

In *A Wizard of Earthsea*, Ursula K. Le Guin uses stately language, reminiscent of much older forms of English, but still easy to understand.

> *"Then he summoned the dragon:*
> *'Usurper of Pendor, come defend your*
> *hoard!'"*
>
> Ursula K. Le Guin, *A Wizard of Earthsea*

Regional accents

In the Harry Potter books, Hagrid has a Scottish accent, but J. K. Rowling suggests it only in some dialogue and in the rhythm of his speech.

> *"Just Ollivanders left now—only*
> *place fer wands, Ollivanders,*
> *and yeh gotta have the best wand."*
>
> J. K. Rowling, *Harry Potter and the*
> *Sorcerer's Stone*

Invented language

Of course, there will always be writers whose sheer inventiveness does let them do things that are outside the normal bounds. In *The BFG*, Roald Dahl invents a whole new vocabulary for his friendly giant. But because the created words remind us, by sound or suggestion, of normal words, we know what he means.

> *"Redunculous!" said the BFG. "If*
> *everyone is making whizzpoppers, then why*
> *not talk about it? We is now having a*
> *swiggle of this delicious frobscottle and you*
> *will see the happy result."*
>
> Roald Dahl, *The BFG*

Social class

Dialogue should also reveal differences in education or social class. In *The Tale of Despereaux*, the Princess Pea sounds very different from the uneducated Miggery Sow.

> *"Soup! Gor! That's against the law."*
> *"Yes," said the princess, "my father*
> *outlawed it because my mother died while*
> *she was eating it."*
> *"Your ma's dead?"*
> *"Yes," said the Pea. "She died just*
> *last month."*
>
> Kate DiCamillo, *The Tale of Despereaux*

Develop tone

In *Artemis Fowl*, Eoin Colfer reverses the usual adult-talking-down-to-child pattern as young Artemis often speaks to the adult Butler as if he were the child. The following three lines give a snapshot of their unusual relationship:

> *"I hope this isn't another wild-goose chase, Butler," Artemis said, his voice soft and clipped. "Especially after Cairo."*
> *"No, sir. I'm certain this time. Nguyen is a good man."*
> *"Hmm," droned Artemis, unconvinced.*
>
> Eoin Colfer, *Artemis Fowl*

Now it's your turn

Pirate talk

Imagine you are eavesdropping on Captain Hook and Smee. They are discussing a host of different ways to kill Peter Pan and the Lost Boys. First, make a list of a few nasty ideas they might come up with. Then think about Captain Hook and Smee as characters. They are both villains, but one is cruel and ferocious and the other more sly. Now write down their conversation, and see if you can give each character his own voice. Invent your own mannerisms if you want to. When you have finished, edit the piece, cutting out all unnecessary words. Then read it aloud and see if it flows. Make more improvements. Dialogue always takes a lot of rewriting.

BEAT WRITER'S BLOCK

Sometimes even the best writers can find they have no words. This is called writer's block and it can last for hours or, sometimes, for years. But what are the causes, and how can you beat them?

Stop the Story Specter

Do you remember the Story Specter, first mentioned on page 9? This is your internal critic who tells you what you have written is no good and eventually drives you back to the television. If this happens, brainstorm some lists or write about your favorite things or the best thing that has ever happened to you.

Trigger new ideas

Another form of block is thinking that you have nothing to say. Again, if you are writing and practicing regularly, you know that you can trigger ideas at the drop of a hat. You are also training yourself to write when you don't exactly feel like it. If all writers waited for inspiration to strike, nothing much would be written.

Now it's your turn

Positive thinking

Write on the cover of your notebook: "Writing is magic, but it is not always easy." Now brainstorm for five minutes, listing all the things you find difficult about writing. Repeat the exercise, only this time list all the things you love about writing. Now look over the problems. Are these things that can be fixed with more time and practice and more reading? Is learning to write more important to you than the problems you are having? If the answer is yes, then give yourself a gold star. You are still on the quest. Your stories will get written.

Rejection or external criticism

No one enjoys rejection or criticism, but they are important parts of learning to be a writer. When you invite someone to see your stories, be prepared for some negative comments. They may be more useful than flattery. You can look at critical comments as a chance to improve and rewrite your story if it really needs it. They become a tool, rather than a cause of writer's block.

Thinking everyone else is a better writer

This is a common trap into which even experienced writers fall. How good a writer you become is up to you and how hard you want to work at it. Only you can tell your stories, and every new one is an addition to the treasure trove of human stories. Read other writers' work to help you improve. Be grateful for their guidance, but don't envy them.

Case study

J. R. R. Tolkien said his story was stuck in the Mines of Moria for a whole year because he couldn't work out what would happen next for his characters. But the long wait was clearly worth it.

Now it's your turn

Try on a cloak of magic

Now, prove you are a writer. In your next writing practice, imagine that you have Harry Potter's invisibility cloak. Use it yourself or let a made-up character discover it. What will you or your character use it for and why? What problems might it solve? What bad effects might it have for others? Will they be humorous or tragic? Tell the story.

When writer's block leaves you stuck mid-story, it usually means there has not been enough planning. Maybe some horrible flaw in your plot has cropped up, and it looks like it is ruining everything. Don't panic. There will be an answer.

Stir your imagination

One way to get around a story block is to play the "What If?" game. Interrogate your key characters in the same way. Build up a web of questions to start finding possible new strands of your story. Some of these could take the story forward in a new way and add some interesting complications.

Role play

Writing is a lonely activity, so why not turn your writing problem into a game with friends or family? Give them character roles to play and see what dialogue between all of you comes up.

TIPS AND TECHNIQUES

Give your character no peace until you know exactly what the quest is. If nothing can spark inspiration for you, you could walk the dog or clean out your bedroom to unwind. Doing tasks that give your mind a rest could be just the thing to ignite an idea.

Keep a journal

Write about life at school or home, and record all the details of your hobbies and interests. Set yourself a minimum target length for each entry, say 300 words. If you use a computer for writing, you can count words easily in your word-processing program. Make a note. Never write less than your target, even if it means describing the pattern on your bedroom wallpaper or what's in your sandwich. But try to write more. And look for ways of turning the day's events into an anecdote. Did your best friend have a spat with her parents? Write about it. Write how you would feel if it happened to you.

Group brainstorming

If your key character is not coming to life, brainstorm with your friends. Start by writing a brief character description on the top of a sheet of paper. When your time is up, pass it to a friend to add his or her ideas to yours. Don't worry about writing complete sentences. Thoughts are what count. When two minutes are up, pass the paper to another person. Mull over the results. Have you learned something about your character that you didn't know before?

Back on Track

If you still think you have absolutely nothing to say, try this. Give yourself 10 minutes to describe the most boring, mind-numbing thing you can think of. Say how you survived the experience. Or maybe you didn't. Maybe it turned you into some other life form that just pretends to be you. Be funny, dramatic, or downright ridiculous. Write it to entertain your friends.

TAKE THE NEXT STEP

Completing your first story is a wonderful achievement. You have started to master your writer's craft and probably learned a lot about yourself, too. But now, you must seek out another quest. Put your first story away in your desk drawer and start a new tale.

Another story?

Perhaps while you were writing the first story, an idea started simmering in your mind. Perhaps you made a few notes in your ideas file. Do those ideas still excite you? Go back to the start of this book and repeat some of the brainstorming exercises to help you develop the idea further. This time around, you have an advantage. You already know you can write a story.

How about a sequel?

When thinking about your next work, ask yourself: Is there more to tell about the characters or the world I have already created? Can I write a sequel and develop the story? Each Harry Potter book, for example, is a complete story, but the characters and the conflicts with Voldemort continue and develop through time and from book to book. J. K. Rowling gives a summary of Harry's back story near the start of her books, so that if someone reads one out of order, they can still understand and enjoy the story. She planned to have a seven-book series right from the start: a book for each year of Harry's training at Hogwarts. In the final book, he will be 17 and a full-fledged wizard.

GETTING STARTED   SETTING THE SCENE   CHARACTERS   VIEWPOINT

Trilogies

Paul Stewart and Chris Riddell's elaborate universe in the Edge Chronicles simply demands to have more tales told of it. A trilogy mirrors the beginning-middle-end of a single story structure, but on a bigger scale. The first book sets the scene, introduces the main characters, shows them in action, solving some smaller dilemma, but then ends with the suggestion of bigger problems still unresolved.

From a different perspective

After completing your first book, you may be bursting to tell the story of one of the minor characters from your finished story. This is another way of writing a sequel. In the Tales from Redwall series and *A Series of Unfortunate Events,* each book is a separate adventure in the lives of the main characters, but the story of those characters' lives runs on from book to book. It is another hook to hold the reader's interest. *The Arabian Nights* is about Scheherazade, who told Sultan Schariar a new story every night for a thousand and one nights because her life depended on it. Each story stopped on a cliff-hanger, as a new one grew out of it. In the end, the Sultan was so hooked on her stories, he canceled his decree to execute Scheherazade and let her live.

As you have found from your own experience, no writer would say that writing is easy. Most well-known writers toiled for years before seeing their first stories in print, and few authors earn enough from their books to make a living.

Why do writers write?

- They write because they feel they must.

- They write to tell a story that must be told.

- They write because they believe that nothing is more important than stories.

- They write because it's the thing they most want to do.

Brian Jacques

Brian Jacques (right) wrote his first story when he was 10 years old. His teacher said it was so good that he couldn't possibly have written it. He left school at 15 and did many jobs—driver, boxer, postmaster, folk singer—but it was when he was a milkman, delivering milk to the Royal Wavetree School for the Blind, that he wrote his first Redwall story to read to the children there. His old English teacher secretly sent a copy of this story off to a publisher, and that is how he won a contract to write the first five Tales from Redwall. His advice: "Be good mice, don't be dirty rats. Remember that television can't take you places the way that books can. So read, read, read."

J. K. Rowling

She wrote her first story when she was 5 or 6. It was about a rabbit called Rabbit, and from then on, she knew she only wanted to be a writer. All the same, it was only when she was grown up and bringing up her own small daughter that she finally finished her first Harry Potter novel. It took her five years to write. This wasn't her first book either. She had already written and put aside two novels for adults. Rowling says, "Being able to say I was a published author was the fulfillment of a dream."

Philip Pullman

Pullman (right) goes to his desk every day at 9:30 a.m. and works until lunchtime. He writes by hand and aims to write three pages of paper. If he reaches this target, he spends the afternoon woodworking or playing the piano. If he hasn't done his three pages, he goes back to his desk until he has. He always finishes his last sentence, or writes a new one, at the top of the fourth sheet—so he won't be faced with a blank page when he starts work the next day. It took him six weeks to write *The Firework-Maker's Daughter* and three years to write *The Amber Spyglass*. He says that "a lot of the time you're going to be writing without inspiration. The trick is to write just as well without it as with. Write only what you want to write. Please yourself."

After your story has been resting in your desk for a month, take it out and have a read through it. You will be able to see your work with fresh eyes and spot flaws more easily.

Editing

Reading your work aloud will help you to simplify rambling sentences and correct dialogue that doesn't flow. Cut out all unnecessary adjectives and adverbs, and extra words like "very" and "really." This will instantly make your writing crisper. Once you have cut down the number of words, decide how well the story works. Does it have a satisfying end? Has your hero resolved the conflict in the best possible way? When your story is as good as can be, write it out again or type it up on a computer. This is your manuscript.

Think of a title

It is important to think of a good title—something intriguing and eye-catching. Think about some titles you know and like.

Be professional

If you have a computer, you can type up your manuscript and give it a professional presentation. Manuscripts should always be printed on one side of white paper, with wide margins and double spacing. Pages should be numbered, and new chapters should start on a new page. You can also include your title as a header on the top of each page. At the front, you should have a title page

with your name, address, telephone number, and e-mail address on it. Repeat this information on the last page.

Make your own book

If your school has its own computer lab, you could use it to publish your own story or to make a story anthology (collection) with your friends. A computer will let you choose your own font (print style) or justify the text (making even length margins like a professionally printed page). When you have typed and saved your story to a file, you can edit it quickly with the spelling and grammar checker, or move sections of your story around using the cut-and-paste tool, which saves a lot of rewriting. Having your story on a computer file also means you can print a copy whenever you need one, or revise the whole story if you want.

Design a cover

Once your story is in good shape, you can print it out and then use the computer to design the cover. A graphics program will let you scan and print your own artwork, or download ready-made graphics. Or you could use your own digital photographs and learn how to manipulate them on-screen to produce some highly original images. You can use yourself or friends as models for your story's heroes.

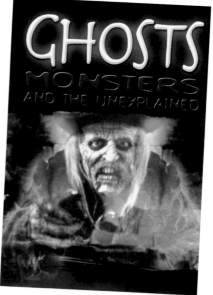

TIPS AND TECHNIQUES

Whether you write your story on a computer or by hand, always make a copy before you give it to others to read. Otherwise, if they lose it, you will have lost all your precious work.

The next step is to find an audience for your fantasy fiction. Family members or classmates may be receptive. Or you may want to display your work to a publishing house or online site.

Find places to publish your story

There are several magazines and a number of writing Web sites that accept stories and novel chapters from young fantasy writers. Some give writing advice. Several run regular competitions. Each site has its own rules about submitting work to them, so make sure you read them carefully before you send in a story. Here are some more ideas:

• Send stories to your school newspaper. If your school doesn't have a newspaper, start your own with like-minded friends.

• Keep your eyes peeled when reading your local newspaper or magazines. They might be running writing competitions you could enter.

• Check with local museums and colleges. Some run creative-writing workshops during school holidays.

Begin a writing club

Starting a writing club or workshop group and exchanging stories is a great way of getting your fantasy story out there. It will also get you used to criticism from others, which will prove invaluable in learning how to write. Your local library might be kind enough to provide a space for such a club.

Find a book publisher

Secure any submission with a staple or paperclip and always enclose a short letter (explaining what you have sent) and a stamped, self-addressed envelope for the story's return. Study the market and find out which publishers are most likely to publish fantasy fiction. Addresses of publishers and information about whether they accept submissions can be found in writers' handbooks. Bear in mind that manuscripts that haven't been asked for or paid for by a publisher—unsolicited submissions—are rarely published.

Some famous rejections

Even though Allen and Unwin had successfully published Tolkien's *The Hobbit* in 1936, the company rejected The Lord of the Rings at first, thinking adults wouldn't be interested. It had taken Tolkien more than 10 years to write. The Hill Company rejected L. Frank Baum's *The Wizard of Oz* because the publisher didn't like the original title, *The Emerald City*. They thought it was unlucky.

If the difficulties of having your work published seem overwhelming, have faith. If you really want to be a published writer, you will find a way.

Writer's tip

If your story is rejected by an editor, see it as a chance to make it better. Try again, and remember that having your work published is wonderful, but it is not the only thing. Being able to make up a story is a gift, so why not give yours to someone you love? Read it to a younger brother or sister. Tell it to your grandmother. Find your audience.

Some final words

Through the magic of fantasy stories, we can explore all the good or bad things that make us human. That is what storytelling is about. It gives us hope. It shows us new possibilities. It sends us on new and exciting quests over and over again.

READ! WRITE!

These are the only bits of writing magic you will ever need.

Case study

Philip Pullman began his storytelling career as a child. He loved comics and used to make up his own stories to tell his younger brother and friends. After a time, he began to write his own stories.

GLOSSARY

back story—the history of characters and events that happened before the story begins

chapter synopsis—an outline that describes briefly what happens in each chapter

cliffhanger—ending a chapter or scene of a story at a nail-biting moment

dramatic irony—when the reader knows something the characters don't

editing—removing all unnecessary words from your story, correcting errors, and rewriting the text until the story is the best it can be

editor—the person at a publishing house who finds new books to publish and advises authors on how to improve their stories by telling them what needs to be added or cut

first-person viewpoint—a viewpoint that allows a single character to tell the story as if he or she had written it; readers feel as if that character is talking directly to them; for example: "It was July when I left for Timbuktu. Just the thought of going back there made my heart sing."

foreshadowing—dropping hints of coming events or dangers that are essential to the outcome of the story

genre—a particular type of fiction, such as fantasy, historical, adventure, mystery, realistic, or science fiction

manuscript—your story when it is written down, either typed or by hand

metaphor—calling a man "a mouse" is a metaphor, a word picture; from it we learn in one word that the man is timid or weak, not that he is actually a mouse

motivation—the reason why a character does something

narrative—the telling of a story

omniscient viewpoint—an all-seeing narrator that sees all the characters and tells readers how they are acting and feeling

plot—the sequence of events that drive a story forward; the problems that the hero must resolve

point of view (POV)—the eyes through which a story is told

publisher—a person or company who pays for an author's manuscript to be printed as a book and who distributes and sells that book

sequel—a story that carries an existing one forward

simile—saying something is like something else, a word picture, such as "clouds like frayed lace"

synopsis—a short summary that describes what a story is about and introduces the main characters

third-person viewpoint—a viewpoint that describes the events of the story through a single character's eyes, such as "Jem's heart leapt in his throat. He'd been dreading this moment for months."

unsolicited submission—a manuscript that is sent to a publisher without being requested; these submissions usually end up in the "slush pile," where they may wait a long time to be read

writer's block—when writers think they can no longer write or have used up all their ideas

FURTHER INFORMATION

Visit your local libraries and make friends with the librarians. They can direct you to useful sources of information, including magazines that publish young people's short fiction. You can learn your craft and read great stories at the same time. Librarians will also know if any published authors are scheduled to speak in your area.

Many authors visit schools and offer writing workshops. Ask your teacher to invite a favorite author to speak at your school.

On the Web

For more information on this topic, use FactHound.
1. Go to *www.facthound.com*
2. Type in this book ID: 0756516390
3. Click on the *Fetch It* button.
FactHound will find the best Web sites for you.

Read more fantasy

Alexander, Lloyd. *The Rope Trick*. New York: Dutton Children's Books, 2002.

Anderson, Janet S. *Going Through the Gate*. New York: Dutton Children's Books, 1997.

Barrie, J. M. *Peter Pan*. New York: Atheneum Books for Young Readers, 2001.

Colfer, Eoin. *Artemis Fowl*. New York: Hyperion Books For Children, 2001.

Collins, Suzanne. *Gregor the Overlander*. New York: Scholastic Press, 2003.

Cooper, Susan. *King of Shadows*. New York: Margaret K. McElderry Books, 1999.

DiCamillo, Kate. *The Tale of Despereaux*. Cambridge, Mass.: Candlewick Press, 2003.

Funke, Cornelia. *The Thief Lord*. New York: Scholastic, 2002.

Ibbotson, Eva. *The Secret of Platform 13*. New York: Dutton Children's Books, 1998.

Jacques, Brian. *The Legend of Luke*, The Redwall Series. New York: Philomel Books, 2000.

Lewis, C. S. *The Lion, the Witch and the Wardrobe*. New York: HarperCollins, 2005.

Pratchett, Terry. *Johnny and the Dead*, Johnny Maxwell Trilogy. New York: HarperCollins, 2006.

Stewart, Paul, and Chris Riddell. *The Curse of the Gloamglozer*, Edge Chronicles. New York: David Fickling Books, 2005.

Tolkien, J. R. R. *The Lord of the Rings*. Boston: Houghton Mifflin, 1993.

Yolen, Jane. *The Wizard's Map*. San Diego: Harcourt Brace & Co., 1999.

Read all the Write Your Own books:

Write Your Own Adventure Story
ISBN: 0-7565-1638-2

Write Your Own Fantasy Story
ISBN: 0-7565-1639-0

Write Your Own Historical Fiction Story
ISBN: 0-7565-1640-4

Write Your Own Mystery Story
ISBN: 0-7565-1641-2

Write Your Own Realistic Fiction Story
ISBN: 0-7565-1642-0

Write Your Own Science Fiction Story
ISBN: 0-7565-1643-9

INDEX

Picture Credits: Alamy: 38 all, 45t, 46t, 56t, 57b. Art Archive: 7t, 9t, 19b, 20t, Bridgeman Art Library: 22r, 48t. Corbis RF: 6t, 7b, 8l, 8-9c, 9r, 12-13 all, 15 all, 17 all, 20b, 29t, 32t, 39r, 48-49c, 49t, 51 all, 54-55 all. Creatas: 1, 4t, 14t, 18t, 30t, 34t, 36t, 40 all, 42-43 all, 44t, 50t, 50-51t, 56 all, 57t, 58-59c, 59b, Dickens House Museum: 14c. Rex Features: 5t, 10-11 all, 16 all, 18-19 c, 21b, 23b, 24-25 all, 26t, 26-27c, 27r, 28t, 28-29c, 30-31c, 32b, 33r, 34b, 35t, 36-37c, 37t, 38-39c, 41 all, 44b, 47t, 49r, 58t, 60-61. Every effort has been made to contact copyright holders of any material reproduced in this book. Any omissions will be rectified in subsequent printings if notice is given to the publishers.